Blank Verse

to dear Sue and Gavin
God bless you and your family

Michael 1/10/2011

To my late, dear, good wife Ruth

Blank Verse

Michael Barrett

Ellingham Press

'Tune' was first published in *Poetry Review*, Autumn 1988, Vol 78.3
'Lumb Bank' was first published in *Singing Brink*, Arvon Press 1987

ISBN 978-0-9563079-8-9

First published 2011

Ellingham Press, 43 High Street, Much Wenlock, Shropshire TF13 6AD

Typeset by ISB Typesetting, Sheffield, UK

Printed in the UK by Bridgnorth Print

Contents

About the Author

Frederick Michael Barrett was born in 1934 in Hammersmith, London, and went to school there at Latymer. He has been in and out of university for much of his adult life, though never as an academic, studying variously agriculture, engineering, arts (OU) and Islamic culture (SOAS). A widower with no family, he is an active member of his local church (CofE) but thinks of himself as a theist rather than as fully a Christian. He has not published a collection before – but hopes yet to be enabled to write concerning evolution, purpose and modern faith.

Acknowledgements

With thanks to Robyn Bolam and Maura Dooley for constructive help in workshops and for advice over several years. Thanks also to Philip Musk for his patience and help with my word processing difficulties. The production of this book has been a independent publishing venture, facilitated by Ina Taylor of Ellingham Press.

Michael Barrett

IRON

The railway bridge at Shalford where it spans
the *Wey*: a nineteenth-century structure – steel
and riveted – whose three isosceles
compose a twenty-metre truss: is small
beside the *Forth* – a thing of match-sticks – yet …

Avoiding London, thirty miles away
the route itself, an arc from North to East
from industry, strategic toward five ports:
a broad valley with a placid stream, the rail
line crosses it obliquely on a bend.

Steel, of all stuff least abstract, utter fact
of Man, of manufacture, echoes yet …
its metal ringing from their hammer blows:
how lusty once their urge and purpose was
who drew the sullen howitzer to France.

The genesis of iron (and from it, steel)
as spent stars flare and quench, is understood:
that elemental iron, not just exists
but forms Earth's massive core is evident
of purpose, meta-purpose – not uncaused.

* * *

Blank Verse

WOMAN ON THE BEACH, Guernsey

We saw this woman on the beach
    she had a fine face; I'd say just past its beauty
    her hair was dark, and slightly red
    she wore it almost to the shoulder.
Her male companion looked a good man;
    they sat a few yards from us, near the cliff.
She wore a loose skirt, to mid-calf, cerise
    her petticoat was white and had a *broderie* edge.
Her sandals were made of six weft straps
    she stood one-legged to put them on
    but when she'd crossed the shingle, took them off
    and carried them, bare-footed to the water's edge.

The moist sand blanches under foot
    it is scuffed up as the toes press forward, striding.
Let inane waves erase such evidence of purpose
    for all their strength, they merely represent
    another power – and that perhaps mindless.

She stood a long while, small and distant
    watching the waves break on the rocks
    and sweep in up the beach, and felt
    them surge around her ankles, and fall back.
The wind drew out her skirt, taut –
    a flag, a triangle of flying cloth.
It made a pennant of her hair.

And, between waves, as their tail ran back
    over glazed sand, she stood reflected:
Reflected, figure and triangles.

* * *

Michael Barrett

MONTENEGRO (for Meliha Osmanovic)

She said in Montenegro that the woods
   in June are full with strawberries, wild and sweet.
The women go with baskets and return
   home, laden – make their kitchens loud with fruit.
And said; we eat that evening all we want,
   the rest, preserve against another time.
Remembered texture – tasty berry pulp
   feels slightly gritty – seeds upon the tongue.
Different from those in supermarkets here;
   that too-red flesh we chew like carnivores:
This is an innocent and special bread.

Also, she said, in Montenegro then
   before the war, our people loved the truth.
They had no guile and what they said, they meant
   and neighbours kept their word although it hurt.
In primal bliss, to speak and hear and learn
   and know how wholesome truth is on the tongue.

I thought, but didn't like to say I thought
   that every people has such lovely myth:
Similar but different – that's its strength
   and value – Montenegro is in the mind.
Remembered or imagined virtue all
   the same is ground for aspiration:
To work and dream, to hope and educate,
   believe that what once was can be again.

* * *

THUMB

Earth spins upon the pivot of my thumb;
　　the Universe, the whole of knowledge, thought
　　and understanding turn upon this hinge.

No other evolution of the meta-
　　carpals into wing or flipper, hoof
　　and paw, however wonderful in flight
　　or action, led to limb so lovely as
　　my hand, and graced it with its nimble thumb.

When down I swung from that last tree, thumb loosed
　　the bough – and gripped a handle, grasped a staff
　　a haft, a helm, a shaft – took hold the stars.

Clever and elegant, he holds the pen
　　against my first two fingers as we write
　　adroitly flexing, swivelled at the wrist;
　　while with the other hand counts syllables
　　and stress, to keep the rhythm of the line.

This mathematic thumb, my tutor, taught
　　me number; how to reckon five to ten;
　　and threes and twelve learned on my finger joints.

It is my metaphoric thumb has made
　　a counterpoint among, between, against
　　and with his four more solemn brothers, played
　　the wag, the wit; has spread the jig or frame
　　on which the mind, the Cosmos, all are knit.

Could Horse have taught itself to count, or Cow
　　perceive the symmetry of right and left?
　　I, at my arm's length have my teacher: Thumb.

Michael Barrett

My hand taught method to my mind, and thumb's
    opposing grip taught intellect to hold
    ideas as objects, to compare/contrast
    to handle information, think in pairs
    rotate the obverse; balance and equate.

Not only left and right, but right and wrong
    good Thumb addresses them; holds parley with
    the four across the chamber of my palm.

Is this his secret, then? – how mind conducts
    affairs of business and of politics;
    that thumb and fingers on the same hand
    in loyal opposition, by constraint
    enabled, give such strength – what strength we have.

* * *

WILLOW TREES, near Swindon

These willow trees are thrown about by the big wind
They scoop space in great arcs, inhaling it
They give the dumb gale its loud and rushing presence
They mark the otherwise invisible air, making it manifest
They show the silver under-surface of their leaves
 and luminate an atmosphere already charged with light
They are reflected, fractured, in the wind-vexed river
They are towers in a docile landscape of meadows and cattle
They, alone, stand against a purple sky, heavy with thunder.

* * *

Michael Barrett

CHINESE

Consider the Chinese
   and how beautiful they are
   with their dark-eyed children
But they are so many
   and so many dead.

But these are live, behind me
   waiting at the traffic lights;
   young man and woman.
I watch them in my mirror
   through intervening surfaces;
   back window, windscreen
And am amazed, from having seen
   so many dead on television
   and photographs in papers.

They clutch and lie half-curled
   poor foetuses, and spill
   into an earth that spawned them
Alive, they have like dead
   immobile, sallow faces
   and their speech like birds.

These are live, especially her
   he watches fixed-eyed
   for the lights to change.
His shoulder moves as though
   to put the car in gear:
The lights are still at Stop –
   he must have run his fingers
   down her thigh – she speaks.
Through glass, and glass, and glass
   I see them smile; at three removes.

* * *

Blank Verse

ARGUMENT 1

My thesis views the private parts of all
    land-dwelling, four-limbed mammals as the same –
    except for us – we're differently arranged.

Since Man became bi-pedal and stood up
    we Humans have re-arranged our carnal parts:
    her breasts have drifted north above the ribs
    his penis, southward to the groin: which shift
    makes fucking face-to-face our usual stance.

Though, more important: face evolves, and mind
    interprets the emotion it portrays –
    so, lofty Man's equipped to understand.

Picture an average mammal – camel, wild
    and domestic cats and cattle, rodents, dogs
    and hogs, their nipples on the belly, and
    the cock, abdominal – all set to mount
    her in that age-old, and successful way.

But what emotion? – since she can't see him
    or he, her – only her clasped neck – that brief
    delight; their pleasure, timeless joy – they gasp ...

We who, alone, embrace front-on have learned,
    and recently (a million years?) rehearsed
    our constant theatre of feeling – face:
    our nimble fore-limbs, freed from standing, run,
    run everywhere, eager and tenderly

Terrestrial animals – those different ones –
    locusts or beetles – we most often see
    seem always mated, mounted male-on-top.

How then has Man been able to upset
    this ancient scheme of things – this apple-cart
    of Eve's – and why evolved so late? Perhaps
    the telling kiss – inhaling face-to-face
    her very mouth and nostrils, her each breath.

This lovely feed-back; inter-mind and -face;
    propels, and seems an engine to fulfil
    some unknown purpose – it both guides and drives.

What if this Mind turned from the Face, toward
    the Cosmos; spoke, and got response and found
    itself in dialogue with one it loves;
    with consciousness, intelligence, imagination;
    came to know: Purpose … and beyond …?

* * *

Blank Verse

THREADS

When you are away so long, good wife
   your absence lets small spiders spin
   fine threads of light across our living room
  (which could not happen, were you here);
One sees them only as some slight draught lifts
   them in the sunlight and they glint.
But, as I move about the house they catch
   my face; I sense their countless filaments
   and as old break, new form – half felt, half thought.
I muse that threads so fine could only touch the mind;
   small things, part-thoughts and soft rememberings
   faint promptings: she was here, and will be – when?
Their sadness is, perhaps, the question asked:
   how certain are we that you will return?

* * *

Michael Barrett

FIRST OF JUNE

Waking this morning, what am I to do?
    it is the first of June and not yet four.
I surface slowly; let awareness, dim
      at first, flicker to thought; my eyes un-clam
      to find the room already palely lit.
And you are there beside me – I extend
      my hand and feel the warm folds of your shift;
      the soft flesh with your moving ribs beneath;
      the whisper of your breathing, regular.
So, what am I to do? but meditate
      that one of us one day must wake alone –
      my hand explore how cool your empty place:
You, stirring in a dream, call out, unheard –
      not reassured that 'everything's alright'.
So, what am I to do, this first of June –
      but think – and let my thought accustom me?

* * *

PLATE TECTONICS – a fable

When the last man died, who could remember the land bridge, myth
Began – of how the islands split and seemed to drift apart;
The sea ate in from either side, despite the walls we built;
Recalled how it was rocks at low tide; how we waved and called;
How the more adventurous young men would swim across, to court
On summer nights, young women waiting on the further beach;
How there were cousins and related clans, whose history
Was ours, whose names we had, although they changed as language
    slipped
Apart – first, vowel sounds – then, consonants – then, meaning lapsed.
Distance exceeded hailing – for the wind, if it carried
Our voice, opposed theirs – so there never could be dialogue.

But sometimes, when the wind was right, we heard their barking dogs –
Ours ears pricked. We saw their lights, their ritual fires
At the same season we had ours. Their cliffs and capes grew faint –
They sank to a distance, as we must have done to them
Below the bowed horizon, where their last cloud cap still fumed.

It was foretold and we believed, that, since the Earth is round
And they departed east, they'd reappear to the west;
Much-changed but long-expected, and first evidenced when cloud
In certain weathers, on the skyline, plumed above the sea.

Our histories had differed: while their forests bred a race
Of varied primates, wonderfully agile wits; our plains
Evolved great herds of ruminants, marvellously camouflaged.
Their lakes and swamps had one time raised a fearful tribe
Of reptile carnivores, which harried humans almost to
Extinction: heroines arose – a caste of shepherdesses
Led the people – are still recalled in names of wells
Of tunes, wild flowers, feast-days, places where they stood and died.
While we some time endured a plague of mind-invaders, who
Took people's sanity; tormenting us with writhing dark
Din, day-long nightmare, false persuasion, stop-less hunger, till
There came a school of passionate philosophers who drove
Them; healing us, themselves were martyred; yet whose names we know
From titles of their works, their maxims, precepts and their laws.

Before approaching mountains came in level sight, men armed
Embarked, adventured in frail ships on dreadful voyages.
As we came close, when gunfire lulled, we heard each other's bells
Their music, carried on the wind, was different from ours –
But lovely. Hubbub – how they cheer when goals are scored
And language works again - and leaps to something understood.

* * *

Blank Verse

RIVER YAR

Of all those northward-flowing rivers on the Isle of Wight
    which empty to the Solent and Spithead as tidal creeks
    the only one that really breached that chalk ridge to the south
    and drained, beyond, a catchment long since taken by the sea
    is that truncated, melancholy estuary, the Yar:
Now lined with yachts; in August, pleasant when the tide is up;
    you'd wince to see those flats in winter when the wind is east.
But look from Yarmouth – looking south one sees the faint
    horizon – there, that pass the river cut before the sea
    outflanked it, took its rear and left that cleft, memorial;
    memorial to that lost, that soft, that murmurous hinterland,
    its streams, its steppe, dew-muzzled herds, perhaps and early man.

I knew a man who lived beside this creek
    enjoying wealth that he'd inherited:
Though honestly obtained and wisely used
    its origin was in his forbears' wit
    their innovation and their people's work:
Creative manufacturing of goods
    themselves creative; a firm world-known
    which now no longer is, except in name.
He lived in style, his house being old and fine:
    this house, his land, his yacht, it seemed his life
    being fed by ancient riches, not his own;
    a wealth well-husbanded but not renewed.

I take my point: that I who speak this tongue
    compose where others wrote before, and sang.

* * *

Michael Barrett

THOMAS HOBBES at a Royal Wedding

(old song – 'The Merry-go-round': *Tournez, tournez, mes personnages …*)

Who is this antique man who cranks the handle of his most
Amazing carousel of painted, twirling, bobbing dolls?
His clothes are sixteenth-century, filthed and torn by civil war
And Any yet he gently smiles, and hums that old song: *Tournez …*

Artificer of complex, huge mechanical device
Whose whole contrivance, stable on its gimbals, slowly turns;
The dolls in great and smaller orbits rise and dip, some swift
On cams and pivots – epicyclics whirring: *Tournez …*

Here comes the bride, in white – as fits a girl in such charade
At least her outer clothes; for what she has on underneath
That is her dresser's secret and the prince's privilege
The showman, stern to see me musing thus, barks: *Tournez …*

Do not approach too close, for fear of seeing plastic, cracked
But dressed in silk and braid, the grimace of a painted smile;
For fear to hear the wheeze of forced breath, drawn through valves
To feel, beneath, impelling mechanism urging: *Tournez …*

While slavering journalists snout for royal garbage in the drains
Stiff bishops mouth the mumbo-jumbo of their spent belief
The merry crowds go round, get drunk, are bawdy but rejoice
A poet feels the levers in his arm write: *Tournez …*

Philosopher of social contract - by which men accept
The comfort of an hierarchic state - the rule of law
Without which mechanism, unconstrained we live as brutes;
Good Hobbes, who winds its handle, smiling, murmurs: *Tournez …*

* * *

ANECDOTE

Imagine a group of men; some eight or ten
   are gathered to discuss a business project;
   some already know each other, others not.
At lunch, relaxed, they chat and laugh, and one;
   a stranger, asks another; an industrialist: Sir
   I'm told there is a mystery which surrounds your son
Would you tell that story? So the great man did.

Some twenty years or so, before, this young man
   who was in his final year at Oxford
   had entered the examination room
   with many others, where he took his place.
And, being issued with the paper, read it and was
   it seems, dismayed to find he could not
   answer even one question. In his distress
He called the invigilator to him
   who, wanting to avoid disturbing others
   around, already writing, and to calm
   the young man, urged him stay and try.
But he would not; he rose and left the room
   he took his raincoat with him as he left
   the building; and was never seen again.

Despite the whole process of search, worked through:
   his family and friends used every means they had
   police did all they could – dragged rivers, dredged pits.
They questioned staff at railway stations, ports
   and airports (though there was not much air
   travel in those days) but there never was response.
Whatever means they could, they used; without success
   the missing man was never sighted in Australia
   nor reported seen in Pietermaritzburg.

Despite the trial of hope, gone through – no word
   that first Christmas, when he might telephone from Peru
   nor family festival when, surely, he would come.
Only, out there, a timeless silence emptying everything
   a dark, unanswering and not-understanding void.

Just as his own mind had gone blank
   he was, himself entered into that vast
   forgetfulness the world has – but not his Dad.

That is the story Mr Turner told; whether the man
   who asked was satisfied, we do not know.

* * *

Blank Verse

MR PAUL CHANNON

Mr Paul Channon sat, weeping in his chair
   he was of a noble family and was immensely rich
   (the head held up, the mouth is open but no cry comes out)
When sorrow strikes it falls the same on them as on us, low.

Mr Paul Channon lay, weeping on his bed
   he was a minister in the government of the day
   (such rapid movement of the thorax and the diaphragm)
But his power and influence could not undo what's done.

Mr Paul Channon knelt weeping, in the pew
   he was learned and, as an advocate, he argued well
   (a strange sensation which, at first, one doesn't recognise)
But no rhetoric, no intellect, could bring back what is lost.

Mr Paul Channon stood weeping, on the grass
   his grief was such as other men before have had to bear
   (it is a kind of rapture where the soul inhales itself)
Though happening to many, is felt only by the one.

* * *

Michael Barrett

COLONEL HARRISON
(executed by evisceration 1660)

The radio question-game –
    identify quotations – asked:
Who said, of whom 'he looked
    as cheerful as any man
    in his condition, could'?
The answer: Pepys –
    who wrote of Thomas Harrison
    soldier, man-of-God and regicide.
It is reported also that he fought
    his captors on the scaffold
    but was held, and …
Oh, the knife-work
    that they were to do.
The audience laughed and clapped
    the game moved on:
But Thomas Harrison abides.

* * *

Blank Verse

UNITARIAN CHAPEL, Godalming

The space enclosed by building is that same
    birds fly in, and the stars; as men inhale
    whose labour heaped these simple walls:
Enclosed and differentiated space
    a shanty to contain a magnitude.
There, is the structure; here, the galleried room
    some chairs, a table, a piano, lights.

Likewisewithwordswhichspacesbothwithin
    thelinesandinbetweenmakelegible
    sometimesthemeaningsiftsbetweenthelines

Often, the meaning's in what isn't said
    the silences more vocal than the words;
    the reader furnishes the room themself.

Likewise this faith, whose lack of doctrine is
    its faith; a space or place in which we grow,
    – religious apparatus put aside.
Starting with God; a theist God of love
    somehow concerned with human life;
    and Human spirit thirsting after God;
    and little else.

They honour Jesus as a man, not God;
    and tell us: look for God within your self.
Theirs seems a binary God: Himself and Man –
    with Man constrained by reason, virtue, love.

Some doubt salvation only of the few
    elect, predestined, and believe we all –
    the worst included (and the Devil) – shall
    eventually be reconciled with God.

They have their saints:
Remember of your kindness, Spaniard, scholar
    Michael Servetus who, fleeing Rome   *(1511–53)*
    to safety in Geneva, wanted to debate

The Nature of the Trinity
   and Deity of Christ, with Calvin
   but was burned, instead.
Some others of them think that God exists
   in our minds, only – so they need account
   for purpose, good, and evil – and think we
Alone, stand upright and responsible.

If this is error, often it's recurred
   and been snuffed out and come alight, again:
In Alexandria first, where Arius taught;   *(c. 250–336 CE)*
   then Italy, Hungary, Poland, Holland, here
   and been put down, and come alive elsewhere.
And ordinary, private thought still leads
   innumerable people to the same
   recurrent error, or resurgent truth.

They hold no creed, and do not question one
   another – 'what do you believe?' – but let
   them be, to seek enlightenment themself.

* * *

LANDSCAPE (RIP: Reverend Michael Brown)

You walk, Michael, through this green delicious landscape, sadly:
　　river, suburban town and pastures, traffic, cattle, wooded hills –
　　or seeming sad.
On seeing you I park my car, and take a path to meet with yours
　　to ask – renew our old acquaintance – ask: why sad?
The path we follow marks the edge of town; a sandstone garden
　　wall, a fence; the tarmac ends and grass begins, and trees.
Along the river, weeping willows, combed out horizontal in
　　a boisterous wind, aspire.
You say you're coming from the council office where you paid
　　your house-tax, disapproving, on the latest day; but then go
　　on to speak of failing health, and that you soon retire.
Electric trains come clattering across our landscape, on
　　the London–Portsmouth line: our brown river swirls toward
　　the Thames and to the sea.
Here, the playground where a mother swings her youngster –
　　higher, higher – and we listen to them shout and laugh.
Here, allotment gardens; note the rich alluvium is dark
　　from showers, overnight; how straight and fresh their
　　vegetable rows – broad beans, shallots.
You say your elder girl's expecting and you're looking
　　forward to a grandchild, soon. We talk of women priests.
Approaching as we do, the church looks strangely flat when
　　viewed against that wooded hill; perspective cramped
　　engraved in two dimensions in an eighteenth-century print.
The churchyard fills the foreground; headstones, leaning
　　this and that way, fall about as though, some
　　while following the sting, we see the joke.
Inside; you know the building well, and how its arched and
　　pillared volumes link; and how, when speaking from the steps
　　your one voice fills its big, unseen, connected space.

* * *

Michael Barrett

STOKE

My fingers itch, from nettles: yesterday
   I cleared a children's grave to read their names:
three hold the pen and, flexing, write: I have
    sensation due to molecules of theirs
    from plants whose root had fed along the bone.

Lost children of a parson and his wife
   their places marked by rose-red granite slabs:
Eric and Amy, Richard; ages 1
    to 5; what fever took them, in that last
    week of September, eighteen sixty-four?

And village children too, no doubt; not named.
September, and the wheat is safely in
    and breaking of the stubble land, begun
    and glowing apples heavy on the tree:
But waste – vain prayer, vain medicine, vain love.

A hundred seasons' weather hasn't dulled
    these stones; their polished surface shines, outlasts
    the sting but, more important: I believe
    Eternal means not only, out of time
But also, out of number and of space.

* * *

FORBURY GARDEN

One day last spring my wife Ruth came home laughing
  with a tale about a little boy and charming mother whom
  she'd met with in the public park, the Forbury Garden;
  unremittent traffic revved and roared – its dull throb numbed.

Around this lovely couple, pigeons flocked for food and
  seeing such large birds, the child delightedly called
  'quack-quacks' but his mother, to correct him, laughed
  'Oh, those are pigeons, darling, they're not ducks.'

Close by, the Abbey gatehouse stands, where, in
  an upper room, in seventeen eighty-four
  the girl Jane Austen went to school: a woman
  much concerned with constancy and truth.

And here, the Abbot, Hugh of Faringdon, was put
  to death; November, fifteen thirty-nine.
New times, new men, new policy empowered the State
  to close the monasteries and to seize their wealth.

Commissioners came, demanding that the Abbot sign
  to legalise the seizure; treason to refuse.
Confronted: God's or Caesar's? – though he tried evasion
  eventually was bound to answer: 'God's.'

And so they brought and ranged against him that whole
  mummery of law: their court condemned him; had him
  executed publicly by fearful mutilation – and his
  Treasurer with him, was of equal mind.

Quit your ranting, diesels; let Saint Hugh be heard
  and shush, you turbines; let Miss Austen speak
  and hush, and heed that gentle mother as she tells
  her youngster: 'Those are doves, son – they're not ducks.'

* * *

Michael Barrett

ABA-NI-JO-RIN

West of Addo in a flat terrain, there is a hill
  a granite *inselberg* two long, and half a kilometre
  wide: an elongated dome a hundred metres high
  that rears sheer-sided from surrounding scrub.
                                           But, at one place
  there's access where you climb the sloping shoulder of the ridge.
The rock is crystalline and, wearing soft-soled shoes which grip
  the gritty surface, you walk with ease along its haunch.

  The motor road swings round the hill, about
  two kilometres distant, in an arc
  so, as you travel past, it does not pass
  but seems to follow, keeping at your side;
  the bush paths, likewise, curve around the rock.

An extraordinary thing about this *island mountain* is
  its broken back – the granite fractured right across the ridge.
Part-way, the bare stone pavement opens at the walker's feet
  a cleft, a metre wide – so narrow you can step across.
A plunging darkness; though one's eyes and mind recoil, they're drawn.
Its edge, unweathered – as though the split was yesterday –
  you walk right to the brink, and learn its angle with your toes.
And gaze down past your feet, and search the beckoning depth, and see
  the brown bats flit and cling there, which our voices had disturbed:
Feel that strange perspective looking down on things flying, gives.

  I asked my neighbour what the hill is called;
  he said: *Aba-ni-jo-rin*. And when I asked
  what that means, he replied: *The rock that walks
  with you*. Why? He answered that the country
  folk who use the paths believe the rock
  accompanies people who revere it, as they walk.

There are two precipices, facing, and a yard apart
  for sure, you'd fall for ever in a darkness, if you fell.
A person, as he steps across might murmur *jesus christ*
  or in some other manner name his God – and trust his guide
And have that whisper echo in his mind … some time.

* * *

Blank Verse

BRONZES (for James Berry)

James, you know these enigmatic sculptured heads, from Ife
    in West Africa, and know how grand they are.
They're brass, in fact – cast by the method *cire perdue* –
    there is no knowledge of this art among the Yoruba, today
    whose sculpture is of stylised carved wood figurines
    and masks: these are naturalistic, portrait heads.

They seem to form a court, a company of dignitaries:
    One, of special beauty, is the goddess Olokun
    or some primordial queen; another, a princess;
    a third woman, some great matriarch.
The rest are male; one, a king –
    perhaps old Odudua, who begat the tribe –
    head and torso, with regalia, wearing beads
    obese, and with the navel carefully formed.

Some other males; ten or twelve life-size heads
    are pierced with pin-holes round the brow and jaw
    apparently for fastening hair and beard.
Some have their faces scarred with close, fine
    parallels, curved to meet below the chin.
Most have a nail-hole in the neck, to fix them
    to a wooden post, or trunk, to function in some rite.

The *lost wax* process, used in making them, is thus:
    beginning with a core of clay, the sculptor
    modelling in wax, would build the portrait head –
    much as thin flesh is laid upon the bone about your face.
This is cased in clay to make a mould, and left to dry
    then heated and the melted wax drained out:
The sculpture – now the void between the core
    and outer clay, into which the molten brass is run.
When cool, the mould is smashed, to bare the casting.
So one, only, of each head is ever made.

James, they would greet you 'Brother, enter and be welcome'
  and, after all manner of courtesy and salutation, ask
'Philosophise – tell us of money, and of what it means –
    No, not accountancy, but metaphysics. And, Jim
    Man, make us laugh – read to us from Lucy's letters home.'
But chiefly, tell us what Man is – what spirit moves him
    that he wrestles in his mind with cause and purpose, laws
    and structure; works metals; embarks on giddy journeys –
He who as a young man stole fire, stole fruit.

* * *

HISTORY OF THE ENGLISH CHURCH AND PEOPLE

These hills were peopled once but now have few; with flocks
    and herds, their crops and orchards – and their strife.
The hills themselves are low and unremarkable
    on maps of Earth this area is shown as plain
    but, even so, there is mild eminence.
It's not so much the height of this above surrounding clay
    which makes a wet and sullen dwelling place
    as that the hills are sand and therefore, dry
    and in that sodden climate, fit for habitation.
Here, villages clustered, cottages and farms
    with each its temple to their ancient God.

Who was, they said, three gods in one; whatever that might mean:
The first, an old man dressed in sheets
                  who wrote a vast dull book, now lost;
And next, a dove which – somehow linked with fire and tongues, we don't
    know how – had agency to act through words and works of men;
Then next, a young man nailed and hanging on a tree
    whose spilled, pretended blood they drank two thousand years
    until this strange creed went the way of all belief.
These strictly should be listed in their ritual order:
    Author, Young man, Wretched pigeon.

The younger man it was, who formed the centre of this cult
    and for his love, his devotees endured the punishments
    of those opposed to them who, for the most part, held
    substantially the same belief.
They had their mouths, eyes, bowels, limbs and private parts
    researched by fire and tongs, traction, presses, hunger, blades.
Not merely endured these things, themselves, but would perform
    these same devotions on their fellows who, in some minute
    degree held different views from theirs.
All for their one-third-God's sake – whose other name was *Love*
    (a quaint emotion which we barely comprehend).

How harsh and merciless a deity! you may conclude –
    indeed, a strange God – yes, but stranger men.

* * *

Michael Barrett

MATTHEW ARNOLD

The sea is wild tonight
The wind blows loud, the air is thick
With spray and rain – an active swirling grey
Dissolves your adamantine cliffs;
Smothers the sea and sky, and works of man;
Blurs the distinction, water, air and earth.
Battered, the senses reel, half-blinded, drenched
Deafened and breathless, almost overwhelmed.
In uproar, grating waves and gravel clash
But balance copes and reason grips.

Scheduled, the ferry leaves its berth
Heads for the harbour mouth, and out;
Straight into heaving grey
Which bursts up, white, above its bow
And sets its course for France.

Yellow in oil-skins, undismayed, two men
Fish from the steep and shifting shingle, right
At the storm edge, but keep their foothold when
Huge waves fling at them, and run screeching, back.
They tend their gear; their rods are firm; their black
Taut lines reach, steady into gibbering surf.
Sometimes, they speak and grin, teeth white
And sip at hot tea from their flask.

The sea of faith is never calm:
Come to the window, Matthew, of your room
The comfort, certitude, the peace there breed
A gothic loftiness of mind:
Turn for an hour, from your bride;
Come to the door, do up your anorak
Be stung by salt, be buffeted by wind
Witness the ocean of religion, rage
And know that they who grapple it
Do so for love, from pitching deck
And raking shingle … with a certain joy.

* * *

Blank Verse

GLASGOW STATION (St Enoch) – since demolished

This empty station, in this dour city serves to drain
their people from the islands and the streets;
this locus of departure in a country of goodbyes.
Enter this great vaulted hall – silent that
imperious crank of locomotives – yet reverberates:
If iron trembles, how much more must we?
and how the heart must sink at that first blast
of parting, pant to purposes beyond our under-
standing, yet to which we have no choice but bend.

Some chocolate from this shuttered kiosk
faded placards advertise the brand
is bought with pennies from her handbag;
let her warm hand melt it slightly, blur
the maker's name through foil – a morsel
on his journey – comfort when the guns begin.

See them enter, marching and, commanded, break
for brief endearments, and embrace those waiting –
how his great boots mock her tiny shoes, who pits
her love against that call which shrapnel has: a
smart-dressed woman cleans a carriage window with
her gloves to gaze some minutes longer on her son.

See, others come in on their own, come randomly but flow
in current nonetheless – clasped hands before long voyages –
enormous distances consume them more than war: who spent
his years in tending engines, that the pumps ran sweetly, that
the levels kept; who might have loved a wife
and cherished children – taught them football and to dance.

And though men, properly, seek success and its rewards
such men are bought, enfeebled by their obvious desert
there is that stoic gift which harder metal failure anneals;
that form of pride which making such an end, redeems itself.
Redemption, not by some last trick that shows their failure as
disguised success: no, utter loss and waste without least hope
of salvage or eventual bliss, but by acceptance of a paradox.

I can no longer speak of them – I have no right –
for they are gone ahead, by this passage, are
already accepted into an intensity – and luminate.

* * *

GANNER

Who Ganner was that his grey photograph was framed and hung
    in Granny's kitchen, set me asking as a little boy: 'Is that dog Jim?'
No, Jim was her rough mongrel whom we romped with in the yard
No, that fine spaniel with his silken ears was not
No, that was Ganner, their employer, Mr Ryland's dog –
    his friend and gun-dog; loyal companion to a sad, wise man.

I must have pestered her: 'Where is he now? what happened t' him?'
    and she perhaps forbore to speak of death to one so young –
To say that he was old and sick and had to be put down – so gave
    evasive answer that she thought might suit a child –
Not lead his questioning – 'Oh, he was very old …' she said
'…they took him to the woods and turned him loose.'

Alone in wilderness – Alone – to fend there for oneself: and though
    the youngster ceased his asking, seeming satisfied, was not –
    her answer set an image running frantic in his mind, some forty years.

I hear your crying out, your panting breath
    your crashing in the thickets of the mind:
Oh, as I call your name, oh, hear and come
    and cease your long purgation; me, my grief.
Come drink and eat, be comforted, be hugged
    and sleep contented at our fire, your head
    lolled heavy on my foot, I shall not move
    to ease my cramp – to not disturb your peace.
Tomorrow, will I comb your burs and mud –
    now, sweetly breathe and dream, and salivate.

* * *

Michael Barrett

DOGS (fragments of wall-painting, hunting scenes, in an old house)

'Ho! Quiet, you dogs; have done! sit, sit; be still'
   grey jostling bodies, limbs; your tails erect
   your warm and panting mouths; those slobbering jaws.

Forgive my dogs! my daft, excited dogs –
   just back from hunting, muddy and so wild
   so merry; bloody, bur-screwed, torn and glad:

Hunting along the Rhone, those bison – leapt
   from the cave wall by our flickering lamp;
   that pierced lion from the *bas-relief.*

Each dawn, the huntsman calls them with his horn:
   they answer and rush, yelping, tumbling out;
   grey, into grey first-light – those mists that lie
   along the royal Tigris, the imperial Nile
   Five Rivers, and the Guadalquivir;
   from hills of Hebron and the plain of Thebes.

I hear them giving tongue; triumphant voice;
   all day, from blue-dyed tapestries, great bear
   wild boar, the stricken antelope brought down.

Then, at late afternoon in fading light
   returning out of time, re-occupy the house.

* * *

LECTURE

We listen in a spacious room, and face
    a window looking east through which the sky
    is huge with distant cumulus, and trees.

The lady speaker cannot see this view:
    the blue-gold sky-scape or the gusting trees
    but just our hundred faces, listening.

While all the hour she lectures aircraft come,
    unseen, unheard by her, from continents
    of cumulus; approaching specks – then planes.

Her lecture title: *Creativity*
    and Criticism; how they interact
    her thesis; that they form a dialogue.

With *Criticism* understood to mean
    appraisal; and Literature, that stock
    of ancient stories common to mankind.

While aircraft, at two-minute intervals
    queued in the distance; small and smaller, black
    approached, took form, their brilliant metal shone.

No author writes in isolation, but
    as member of a long continuum;
    from Greece, and those unknown before the Greeks.

Plane after plane became, behind her head;
    invisible at first, a speck, a seed
    a fuselage that grew, then engines, wings.

In ceaseless murmur of those tales, reworked
    as when *King Lear*'s retold as *Mansfield Park*
    the psyche finds a bass, a base, a ground.

These planes, such traffic, touching tree-tops, tip
    a parapet; appear as from her brow;
    and pass from sight, with each its freight of souls.

Her thesis; each creative work contains
    like stardust, an ancestry of reference;
    the human spirit contemplates itself.

This is distraction from her voice and what
    she says: the still-young woman, crimson dress
    with ruby ear-rings, lightly wears the gown:

In essence; there exists in literature
    community of witness: liberal, true
    not-secret, and immortal colloquy.

* * *

Blank Verse

ENGLISH GRAMMAR

It must have been the Isis or the Cam
    in which that German drowned who got it wrong:
Confusing 'shall' and 'will', in his distress
    he cried 'I vill drown, and no-von shall save me'
    so, passing scholars, taking lack of gram-
    mar for determination, let him sink.

At school they used this tale to teach us kids
    the different use of 'shall' and 'will'; I grinned
    to show I understood – but never did.

Another's grammar likewise failed him when
    he struggled, choking in some foul canal.
A passer-by who heard, threw down the pack
    he carried, offed his steel-shod boots and called
    'Yo poo-er bügger, A'll not let thee droon'
    and dived, and pulled him to the bank.

* * *

Michael Barrett

GULLS

I see them flying still, in my mind's eye, those gulls
    of former time, dimly, to the upper left as from
    my window, looking east; dim, not for lack
    of certainty but because the sweeping snow obscures
    them – they emerge a moment and are gone.
Come in off the North Sea, the wolf-grey ocean, they
    appear singly, hang briefly, while huge snow flung
    round them: ask, how many gulls? I cannot tell
    but guess; so many, many gulls.

The snowstorm took them with it and, when the drifts
    had thawed we didn't find a single carcase – Time had
    taught them; flight in snow provides the only shelter
Something to do with aerodynamic forces on the wings
    how lowered pressure on their upper surface sweeps
    them clean – I guess they have no pleasure – don't fly
    in falling snow for fun, or for its beauty, or for profit
    since it seems a most unlikely place to seek for food.

Those who had not learned were leaded down
    without ancestral knowledge, fall
    are at a great depth and are sinking still.
These sail, these trim and ride the barely habitable air
    with umpteen million years' experience, they keep
    their horizontal flight against its plummeting.

I sometimes wonder if I really, or if I merely
    thought I heard them mewing as they flew.

* * *

LUNAR

In broad daylight
    the pallid moon
    hangs; unable
    to fade.

That face
    we call the 'man';
    only shadows
    cast by mountains.

Its light
    is not its own
    incandescence;
    but reflection.

Of what there is
    some part we see;
    the rest
    our eyes impose.

What is for real;
    it draws
    up-brimming tides
    bulging ocean.

What's more
    it touches us;
    our minds drawn to-
    ward disclosure.

The man-face blurs
    and continents
    emerge;
    all silvery blue.

See: Africa
    and South
    America were
    once one piece.

Michael Barrett

Scandinavia
   mainland Europe;
   peninsulas
   islands.

Who ever thought
   O God
   that it was all
   to do with hurt?

See: square Spain
   there Italy
   and former
   Yugoslavia.

Pale, loitering
   witness;
   who cannot sleep
   for what she's seen.

* * *

Blank Verse

OFFICE

My colleague has, hung on her office wall
Three things which mark the flight of time:
    a clock, that tells her seconds, minutes, hours
    a calendar, to show the days, and weeks, and months
    a mirror, where she may regard her lovely face.

* * *

Michael Barrett

TRAWSCOED

This is a late house of a late period where fine
   materials and workmanship were spent on poor design;
   where architect and patron disappoint the artisan.
But that apart, this house (with its inhabitants) which stands
   in hilly landscape, by a river vocal over stones,
   within a grove of ever-sounding beech, of airy shade,
becomes thereby a place of some delight.

So, enter here by the principal doorway, a low ante-room
   and, seeing no-one – only glass cases containing nothing –
   find, beyond, a spacious hallway with a flight of stairs;
Static but implying movement. But still no-one, for on
   this golden afternoon the house is emptied to the green
   and docile park, and that more distant landscape and the sky.
How yearningly, from open windows billowing curtains pull
   and at a closed pane, an iridescent fly frets.

But on this staircase, at the very centre, presences
   emerge from air or, being here always, now are felt:
Who would not wish to see those slender ladies, dressed
   in ribboned gowns, come splendid down in passion or in hope;
   or grieve to see their slow ascent, distressed
   with lowered head, to upper rooms, to weep?

Yet one might hear their laughter or their whispered stratagem;
   their earnest speech, in voices hushed – the tone but not the word.
Behind closed doors, their dialogue of question and response
   of taunt and protestation, carried on the vacant air.
Soft movement, footfall everywhere and, almost silent, that
   piano, distant, pensive, sweet persistent; and the violin:
Uncertain whether these were heard or were remembered notes.

But they are gone, are gone long since and never can return.
The sound of wheels on gravel took them and they are no more;
   across the sunlit forecourt to the nearer shade, along
   with gathering speed, the drive, this avenue or colonnade
   of static trees – unmoving yet implying motion; cool
   this undershade – all murmurous of leaves and quaking grass.

* * *

ROOM

We had a room once, our living room, or parlour
    which had two windows looking west, like eyes
    across the rooftops (our flat was on the second floor)
    to a splendid tower; Victorian gothic, Gilbert Scott
    brick and stone; St Mark's, in Leamington.
Which has a fine clock that strikes
    the hours strongly and the quarters sweetly
    and, for bells, it has the most
    amazing carillon of ting-tangs
    which make the brides' eyes sparkle
    and the grooms' pace quicken to the car.
It also has one slow bell for those who are no more.

Our windows gazed out on a great sky-scape
    and trees – we couldn't see the church clock-face
    for leaves in summer; just the tiled roof
    of the nave and chancel, and the tower
    with its coronet of pinnacles and open arches.
These were topped with copper crosses;
    judicious blend of science with faith;
    whether sacred lightning ever struck
    I cannot tell, but they make good perches
    for the crows who flop and croak
    and make those parapets their lofty world.

The tower changes colour with the daylight;
    and distance – is near at morning –
    stands back at evening when in silhouette –
But this is to digress …

Our neighbours' roofs were slate
    and on a clear night, the marble moon
    would light them, make them look moist
    though they were dry; seem frozen in a heavy swell;
    or tears for quarrymen whose lungs were choked.
Beyond their roofs' horizon, to the west
    was Warwick; further, the Atlantic which
    begot us, and still reminds us – sending gifts
    of gales and cloud, of rain and cheerful mist.

And often, great furnaces of coloured sunset
   swinging back and to, between the solstices:
   in June, north-west, beyond the church;
December, in the branches of a huge acacia tree.

Once, in summer, when the sun was low
   I saw it beam right through the chancel
   windows; golden, like – I can't say, what.
This, also, is digression from our room, whose
   two windows gazed out onto a modest street.

Sometimes, the room felt carried on my shoulders
   and me inside my head, and looking out
   its two windows, as my eyes.
I sometimes think the world with all its objects
   action, colour, clamour, shines in through one's sense
   projects its images, criss-crossed, some faint:
   I feel them shining on the inside of my head.

Often, if I couldn't sleep at night
   I'd go into this room, and
   not switching on the lights
   draw back the curtains
   and open the Venetian blinds, to let
   the light of many street lamps stream in;
   throwing patterns, paired parallel sets
   of light and shade, cast by the blind slats
   on our whitened walls and ceiling.

First, the lamp outside Bob Kitchen's yard
   some thirty metres to the right, threw oblique
   parallels on our left side wall.
Then, to the left, the one beyond the Perkins' gate
   cast slanting patterns on our right-hand wall.
There were so many grids of parallels
   bright, criss-crossed, faint and fainter
   as the further lamps recede.
A breeze, unfelt by me, vibrates
   the branchy shadow of a tree.

Blank Verse

One evening, when I'd set the blinds and curtains
    I led my wife into the room to share this marvel;
    she came, she smiled, she said:
It's just the shadows which the street lamps make.

* * *

Michael Barrett

LONGUE ROCQUE
a megalith in Guernsey

When would the sparrow, held in the talon, stop
    its fluttering and its calling out?
When the hawk had done, and is again circling
    leaving on top this granite pinnacle, adhering shreds
    of down, which the wind agitates.

The road, west, reaches the brow and, here, the outlook
    opens to the coast; its reefs and inlets.
Nearer; fields hedged with banks; wind-bent scrub
    and – missed except by those who are driving slow
    and looking for it – the standing stone.

Occasional aircraft, turning over the sea, align
    and come in. Wind whistles in the telephone wires.

This piece of unworked stone is not remarkable:
Its shape irregular – it measures almost five metres long
    and roughly one-by-one, across. Only, it stands upright
    – put there – otherwise is unremarkable
It is not possible to say, when – perhaps three thousand years
    but no-one knows – or its function – only later folk-tales.

The knowing biped stood it up: themselves, with nerve
    and sinew, balancing in upright posture, stood it up.

Close to, it occupies the sky; is crusted with dry grey
    algae, with whorls of yellow lichen.
One place juts, where cattle scratch – it is marked
    with their grease.

As you walk back toward the gate and to the car
    turning frequently to be sure – it dips below the sky-line.

* * *

LUMB BANK

Since this window hangs
 or so it seems, out
 over a steep valley
I levitate, and trees
 below my feet, touchable
 though leafless, are
Robust weeds which
 I might uproot
 shake, and throw down
If it were not for my
 kindness to birds which
 build their nests therein.

Magpies dangle below
 and are conspicuous;
Crows, bringing twigs
 bicker lyrically.

A man walking a dog
 on the lower path
 moves distantly and slow;
A grain of sand aimed
 from this height
 would crater him;
But I am merciful.

My hidden stream which cut
 this steep defile, still works
Is audible, and is cold
 to my toes when I reach down.

If I were to shout
 of my pleasure at these things
 there would be rockfalls
Tearing up of forest
 and broken birds' eggs:
 so I will confide.

* * *

Michael Barrett

NEW ROAD

A new road is driven through older districts of the town;
 it cuts across modest streets, whose ends are then walled up;
 truncated houses are buttressed against the void their neighbour left;
Mrs Wurrod can be heard no longer, raking out her grate.

It was similar at St Pancras when they built
 the railway – took half the churchyard:
Mary Wollstonecraft's and William Godwin's bones
 were moved to Bournemouth.

Few, and fewer can remember when the streets ran right across;
 they see the school roof they attended as a child;
 the church, whose bell they hear when the wind is in that quarter.

It is clear, on maps and from the air
 how earlier patterns were cut, across:
The route the wagons took, to the coal-yard, fetching;
 the carters urging, shouting before daybreak:
Hooves strike spark, the wheel rim steel
 screeches on granite; the round dung steams.

I drive along, and am glad of the new connection:
 their houses hang, unhealing at the fracture.

* * *

BLACKBIRDS

Their black is unequivocal: I accept what Darwin wrote
    but why aren't these beige and speckled, coloured, barred
    and crested, different back-and-belly, like the rest?

To evolve, or to have chosen such a suit of feathers
    from the rack of possibility, and to offset
    it with that yellow beak, was brilliant: while the hen
Beautiful and womanly, is dark and single-minded brown.

If they were rare, then men would come
    from Earth's four corners just to hear
    the fabled blackbird, and to see him
    and the amorous hen for whom he sings.
Not so; they nest in every bush, and feast
    on fruit, and pounce for worms on every lawn.
They bathe delightedly in puddles, dip
    and flap and splash in every water bowl.
I hear his voice from every television aerial
    though heaven knows what crap they watch, below.

A map shows distribution: all of Europe, Russia to the Urals
    Turkey, Persia, through Kashmir, Nepal and into China.
From his first singing at dawn, where Peking man heard it
    to his last notes at evening in Ireland, out-pacing time.

They nested, so it's said
    along the trenches, sang
    between shell-fire; sane
Among the world of men.

Their eggs are blue, but spattered brown; little low heavens
    smirched with dung; something of humanity about them.

I find him dead, and think uncharitably
    that Jeoffry, the cat, has sprung him.
Blunt maggots knead him till his fine
    and structured bones are cleansed, by festering.

This hollow of his perfect skull
    smaller than my finger-end, once held a whole:
    his lineage, his mates and rivals, roosts
Places where he fed and drank, morning
    autumn, purpose, flight, the art of bathe-ing
    and that music which makes him organ to an urban world.

* * *

TOAD

In Carboniferous times his people, the *Amphibia*
   had been great lords, of all those vaporous swamps;
      some were huge and crunched two-metre dragonflies like gnats.
And how the forest trembled at their wrath, it echoed
   with their grunts, and rang with trumpeting;
      it stood in awe to see them clasped in vast, slow acts of love.
And, being trodden down and drowned, their rivals stank;
   the chemistry of their flesh is somewhat different from ours
      but, even so, there's no mistaking when they rot.
They sank, still dreaming, in the fossilising silt.

The toad, himself, we met one summer afternoon
   as he came legging it across the lawn, disturbed
      by mowing, making for the sheltered shade of plants.
And crouched there thinking anciently, ancestral, rapt
   yet patient as our fingers felt how pliable and cool
   his skin: goodness and wisdom round his head,
   his jewel eyes, his pierced nostrils which
   convey sweet breath into his pumping throat.

When next we saw him; as a prince transformed – to disadvantage;
   for, having clambered, seeking moisture in our watering-can
   could not get out and, when the sun came round
   was cooked alive. There followed flies.
And when I shook him out and turned him with my toe
   his belly broke in liquefaction of the flesh – such stench
   and pulsed with lively maggots, pure as pearls.

I saw what strange thing Nature; that it can
   in such corruption find a wholesomeness.

* * *

SAHARA

There is this one enormous tree
   stands in the desert, quite alone
   they showed it in a television documentary, once.
Whose roots, they said, reach down
   into fissures in the underlying rock
   where, at great depth, there's water.
It is a relic, so they told us
   of a grove – hardly a forest
   of *Cupressus* which throve there, long ago.
Until the spreading desert overwhelmed
   them, bar this one.
The rest were smothered by the drifting sand
   and no more saplings grew, replacing them
   they were so parched.
It lingers still, still draws
   from that same aquifer, is scorched
   but sows seed to the arid ground.
While, round it, day and night, moan
   alien winds.

* * *

CAR PARK

A woman with
her clearly Jewish mother parks her car
near mine; I watch but cannot hear them talk
but guess her '... back in twenty minutes, Mum'.

I watch the younger woman; note her smile,
the high bones of her cheeks; and guess she has
a husband – or a lover – maybe, both
and three dark-eyed, already-clever kids:
their Friday evening meal, together – bread
and herbs, their candles, teaching and the law.

I note her dress; its quality, its style
and colour – apricot; her raincoat – tan:
she goes on business; while the other waits.

Waiting, she eyes the dash displays and dials;
Outside, grey rain recalls a childhood flight;
Far lyric fountains plash in sunlit courts.

Etched *'safety'* and *'security'* on glass;
Remembered vomit of her journey here;
Imagined honey of that promised place.

The wiper blades have marked the glass with arcs;
Flies' countless bodies emptied on the screen;
The ark of beaten gold – the holy box.

I have an impulse – but at once hold back –
this fresh-baked shortbread – give it. It is wrapped
for giving (though to someone else) – of white
wheat flour and butter, tang'd with lemon. What
wild impulse! What absurd emotion! – take
it, walk across and, mumbling, offer it.

Impossible! She knows our faith of old –
about that tower in York – so, would decline;
not winding down her window, shake her head.

Michael Barrett

What if: feeling myself misunderstood –
my motive suspect – in anger I
let slip that I am understood ... too well?

* * *

WALTZES

1.

One recent evening, someone put a CD on
    of Chopin waltzes – so our precinct rang
    with sudden music.
Neighbours, mesmerised by television, woke;
Others, studying for examinations, sighed;
Mothers, cooking, paused a moment, felt inspired.
One couple, having sex before their supper
    were distracted from their passion by the lyrical
    piano, and forgot – their soufflé burned.
Some bloke, washing cars, was lost in rapture; let
    a running hosepipe flood a Rolls.

Frédéric Chopin, we are hoping that the man's
    insurance policy will pay:
Meanwhile, Tamás Vásáry will play.

                                    * * *

2.

Rebecca telephoned to say she cannot
    come on Friday.
Meanwhile, in the background, someone playing Chopin
    on a record.
Playing Chopin, with a passion, plays a waltz
    and then another.

'Rebecca, though you're thirty kilometres
    distant …' – I feel my arms
    embrace her and the room begin to spin.

                                    * * *

Michael Barrett

TUNE

Sing me that tune they danced to in the play, last night
   those eight young people coming, as they did
   to four marriages. It was serious fun – we smiled.
While through misunderstandings in the plot, the characters
   reveal themselves; the wise, the overbearing and
   the frivolous, the good – and find their match.
The music helped us sense the joy they felt, and their
   solemnity, before their lives began outside the play.

It was a tune I hadn't heard before but now won't leave me
   it goes on playing in my head, but when I want to hum
   or whistle it, cannot – it does the same for you.
You've sung it several times around the house, today
   and when I called 'You've got that tune!', said
   'What tune?', 'That one they danced to in the play'.
And when you tried to sing it, couldn't, any more than me
   we try again – dee, da, di-di, da, da – but it has gone.

Quite soon, the bass creeps back, and pulses – near where
   the head is balanced on the backbone – and is palpable.
Where, one might imagine, mind and body meet; if any place.
There is something of carnality about the bass; the melody
   is airy – ethereal, perhaps – though how
   would spirit show itself, without incarnate things?

The rhythm goes on throbbing, somewhere, while we snatch
   at the melody – but can't catch it – as it comes and goes:
   it is a kind of knowledge which we have – though we forget.

Remind me of that tune they dance to in the play.

* * *

RAILWAY

She had described how, on a tight bend
    in a mountainous terrain
    where the line looped back upon itself
From a front carriage of the train
    creeping to negotiate the curve
    one might look across a valley
And see the rear coaches
    with people in them, moving
    in the opposite direction
Though on the same train
    on the same journey
    and how strange it seemed.
She had drawn it with her finger
    on the counterpane, in explanation.

I have her photograph
    head and shoulders, a framed
    portrait, posed at 19 Westgate Road.
Browned by a hundred years
    dramatic hat, and a good face
    the bodice of the time recedes.

After her long voyage south, to Cape Town, as a young wife
    she spent her early womanhood at a small settlement
And, being widowed, somehow found for her two sons
    (one of them, my father) and brought them up
With much kindness from neighbours
    and magnanimity of natives.

There are the usual stories of snakes; how, there
    the starlings' wings are tipped with scarlet
Of fearful storms and lightning strikes; how
    sudden floods can rise in gullies, can sweep
    away the travellers and their horse.
That was in a time of war, and when they made
    the journey to the rail-head and to Pietermaritzburg.

Michael Barrett

From the rear coach of the train in which I travel
    I look across the valley she described
To a forward carriage, where, framed at a window
    a pretty woman in an Edwardian hat is sitting
    perhaps embroidering crimson wing-tips
And watch, half hope, half fear she may look up
    and smile – and I should understand.

* * *

This poem relates to 'Passengers' by Robyn Bolam (aka Marion Lomax).

STORY

This story which I tell, though it concerns
    is not about, a clergyman: it starts
    with filth and moves in some degree toward grace.

Beside the Rectory gate was not a place
    even at night and taken short, a man
    would put his trousers down and defecate.

Yet, stool there was; too big to be a dog
    there, plainly, by the Rector's path, right where
    his wife and kids walked on their way to school.

Most likely, someone brought it there for spite
    and put it as an insult by the gate;
    to salve some real or some supposed offence.

So many people; friends, parishioners
    and weeks went by; we, no-one chose to see
    or cleanse, but passed by on the other side.

And why did not the priest himself – not come
    through pride – through choosing to endure – not come
    some quiet time, alone, and clean it up?

At last, some unknown person who at times
    had gone that way and vaguely thought 'why me?'
    for shame had fetched a trowel and buried it.

Its only stink, a whiff of phenol, showed
    attempt to neutralise misguidedly
    served merely to perpetuate the thing.

Though be that as it may, the point remains:
    a trespass of such weight, a man can not
    lift off his back himself; but needs an advocate.

* * *